YELLOW ARROW

Vol. VIII, No. 1
Spring 2023
Kindling

Yellow Arrow Journal

Creative nonfiction, poetry, and cover art by writers and artists who identify as women

Vol. VIII, No. 1
Spring 2023
Kindling

Editor-in-Chief
Kapua Iao

Guest Editor
Matilda Young

Editorial Associates
Jackie Alvarez-Hernandez, Angela Firman, Siobhan McKenna, Natasha Saar, Beck Snyder, and Rachel Vinyard

Contributors
brooklyn baggett, Jessica Berry, Helen Chen, Emily Decker, Zorina Exie Frey, Violeta Garza, Amanda Hayden, Yuemin He, Raychelle Heath, Cori Howard, Nancy Huggett, Tess Kay, Al Kelly, Thomasin LaMay, Michelle Levy, Susan Mack, Annie Marhefka, Sarah McCartt-Jackson, Kathleen McTigue, Sarah Piper, Jude Rittenhouse, Mandy Shunnarah, Psyche North Torok, Janna Wagner, Katharine Weinmann, Kathryn Wieber, and Ellen Zhang

Cover Art
Violeta Garza

YELLOW ARROW
PUBLISHING

PO Box 65185, Baltimore, MD 21209
info@yellowarrowpublishing.com

Yellow Arrow Journal - Kindling
Copyright © 2023 by Yellow Arrow Publishing
All rights reserved.

ISBN (paperback): 979-8-9850704-7-7
ISSN (print): 2688-3015
ISSN (online): 2688-3023

Cover art by Violeta Garza (violetagarza.com).
Cover and interior design by Yellow Arrow Publishing.
For more information, see yellowarrowpublishing.com.

Inheritance
Al Kelly

I am the answer
to my ancestor's whispered prayers.
Baby, my rest is divine.
And my breath,
my breath,
my breath
is revolution atomized.

Table of Contents

Dear Readers,

There is no one way to heal the world; the only requirement is that we try. There is so much darkness in the world, but even the smallest spark can start a fire.

For the spring edition of *Yellow Arrow Journal*, we asked writers to submit their work around the theme of **KINDLING**. The artwork, poetry, and creative nonfiction we received were illuminating and inspiring. Our incredible cover artist (and poet), Violeta Garza, captures the theme beautifully in her cover art as well as in her artist statement: "I see kindling as the grouping of individual pieces that, with enough chemistry and action, create an explosion." The pieces we showcase on the following pages speak to the intersectional nature of our struggle to build the world we want to live in, the future we want to make possible.

In this journal issue, the writers we feature talk about people's connections to one another. Sometimes, these connections are familial. Sometimes they are communal or based on identities we hold. Sometimes they are born of kindness, or suffering, or random chance. However we find each other, by coming together, we can learn something about ourselves and the world around us. We can learn that we are not alone, that we can be loved, that, as Kathleen McTigue writes in these pages, we can find the world's "deep heart still there beating." And that knowledge has the possibility to be transformational.

The pieces within **KINDLING** are also works of bearing witness. James Baldwin once wrote that "not everything that is faced can be changed, but nothing can be changed until it is faced." Through their art, the **KINDLING** creators force us to grapple with painful injustice and with the oppression that surrounds us and the oppression that we are complicit in. They ask us to remember the people we could not—would not—save. And they ask us to look at what we can do to help right some of these wrongs.

The pieces here also contain visions for paths to brighter days ahead. As adrienne maree brown famously wrote, "all organizing is science fiction. we are bending the future, together, into something we have never experienced." In this issue's pieces, writers imagine how we might bend the world toward justice, toward authenticity, toward empowerment, toward community care, toward joy.

These are writings steeped in love. These are writings filled with purpose. And in so many ways, they remind us that the kindling can and must start with us. Within her poem explaining the root causes behind civil unrest in the Black community, Zorina Exie Frey asks us to "Look how fierce I've become." The power to change the world is within each of us—our fierceness, our strength, our love, our creativity, our truth. And together, as Nancy Huggett writes in her aptly titled poem "Kindling," "we [can] build the nest bigger."

In solidarity,

Matilda Young

Matilda Young
Guest Editor

KINDLING

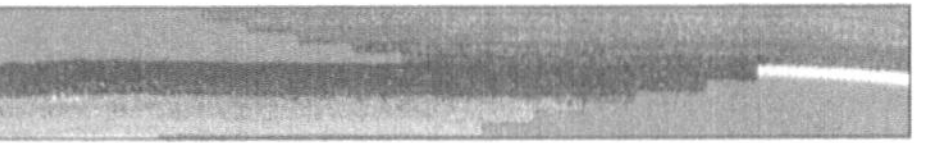

CALLING
Sarah Piper

Put down the phone.

You don't need it now.
This winter of barren, white cold,
of snow-blind eyes and masked moons,
of ice-sheet roads in every direction—
this time of waiting out the storm—
is receding with a trickle of snowmelt
through the rocks underfoot.
A tinkling like delicate and
dazzled voices whispering *now* and *go*.

Put down the phone.
The winter birds are waking early,
cutting silence with song—
melody born in black, this long night
yielding to the stage of morning.
They sing of all mornings, everywhere.
And no one else can hear
your morning, can know
the lessons of your night.

Put down the phone:
today, the first day of *possible*,
the first of daring, dogged days,
there is no one to call to ask
where to put your next foot in the snow,
which blank canvas to head toward,
to settle at and on your knees,
to begin painting a different landscape
for a different sky.

For the task of turning time—
a new vision for a harsh season,
a revolt and a remembering—
there is no need to wait
for the globe to spin by degrees.
The season of vivid, hot light is within you:
there is no one to call for permission
to unzip your jacket and
let it burn new lines on the world.

› # *wom·an /ˈwo͞omən/ verb*
Annie Marhefka

1. To woman is **to sing**, her voice a trilling on the tails of the wind's gust. Her sound reverberates like the echoes of a thousand tired mothers passing cautionary tales down across generational divides, stirring spices into earthy stews and scribbling down secret recipes meant only for daughters. Her song simmers to a whisper, a tiptoeing around the jagged crags, a solemn patience, a waiting. Her crescendo comes from the depths of her, the diaphragm swelling up into a sensational tremor; a roar emerges into the crisp of the night.

> *In the beginning, we wake in three-hour intervals to feed. She latches frantically; I sing to calm her, to set the pace. She doesn't know much in this world, but she knows the tone of my voice; she knew it from within, a muffled, watery version of my crooning. She sways with me, her body cradled in my arm. They call it a football hold, the way the infant tucks her head into your palm, her bottom nudged into the elbow's crook, but it doesn't feel that firm or stable or sure. It feels like you're bursting through the line of scrimmage, rattling bones and bouncing off skulls and wearing down the body one collision at a time.*

2. To woman is **to nurture**, to absorb the invisible burdens of those around her, soak their achiness into her skin, the woes stuffing her pores until she is so bloated with empathy she forgets her own self. Her gut instinct is to protect, a frantic doe leaping in front of a car to save her young fawns, the weight of her synapses firing off anxieties heavy on her chest, a cast iron worry corset. Her arms latch onto another's, holding firm to her kinship. She stands with her, marches with her, scales a fence with her. She bleeds with her. She uplifts. She says: *I am here.*

There was that spring break in college when we rode in her Volkswagen together with the windows down, even though it wasn't warm enough, and ate chicken cheesesteaks and sang along with Macy Gray as loud as we could. It was a cold spring again 10 years later when I had shown up at her apartment tugging a suitcase, the last days of a marriage behind me. I tried to tell her why I was there, but she knew. I recall the way she tucked my hair behind my ear, found the old Macy Gray CD in a dusty bin in the corner, put on that song about trying to say goodbye and choking, turned the volume up until I couldn't help but sing.

3. To woman is **to taste** the earth, lick its savory roots, sprout blossoms from beneath its bark, shed delicate petals, coat the ground in a blanket of silk. You may think you see her sway, but the roots of her are dug in deep; they claw beneath the surface. Her trunk stands firm while her boughs mold gentle fruits of tangy pinks and zesty yellows. You only ever notice the fruits.

There was that time you messaged me, said we should catch up and so we grabbed lunch and you saw my swollen belly for the first time because I had been afraid to tell you how I was pregnant because you were not, again. And we twirled our spinach leaves around forks and poked at the feta crumbles and tasted the tartness of the balsamic, and you talked about how you were jetting off, again, somewhere else exotic, and I told you I wished I could jet off, too, and you said no, you don't.

4. To woman is **to woo**, to emit aromas of lush lavender and vanilla, let them curl through eager nostrils, let them linger. Her scent is thick with pleasure, an ecstasy; a trace of it makes you shiver with anticipation. It enchants you, makes you forget what you came here for. It erases you.

These days, there are soft touches like a coffee mug on my bedside table when I wake, a hand brushing my shoulders as

I nurse the baby, a whisper about having taken care of that bill I'd forgotten. But once, we weren't soft; we were hard and sharp and pulsating. Like that night at the Irish pub with the late-night DJ in the back when I leaned into you and our feet suctioned to the floor where all the dancing couples were sloshing drips of Jameson and ginger and we had to pry our feet up from the tiles, ricochet off each other for air. I relished the way our bodies clung to the impermanence of the night, the way our lips held the moment in a hush.

5. To woman is **to crack**, to split open the facade and expose the vulnerable innards, to weep of what it is to woman. Her bark is rough and hardened to the elements she encounters, but within she is tender. She says: *I'm fine, I'm fine, I'm fine,* and you laugh and tease about how she never really means it, but she must say it because if she doesn't hold the line of fine, everything crumbles, disintegrates into dirt. It all collapses without her. She holds it all in check with her calm.

> *Sometimes I feel I am seething, the pressure of the pushing back and the pushing down all just too much to contain in one body. I wonder if I am foaming at the mouth, a hint of what's hidden behind thin lips. Chapped. Bubbling. Sometimes I wonder what it would be like to just let it all erupt.*

6. To woman is **to ignite**, but not in the way you'd think. She doesn't erupt unexpectedly; no, she plans. She quietly tends to the foundations of things, she works to stoke, stoke, stoke the fire, and waits until the wind catches just right. The embers sear her skin and singe the wispy hairs; they melt into her. She never takes her focus off the hearth, though. She waits. She endures.

To woman is **to blaze**.

Rachel Carson Wildlife Refuge, Maine
Amanda Hayden

We saunter along her sea breath nests
her refuge of migratory waterfowl
her treasure of a place, warm inhale of
pine needles, salt marsh, kestrel hawks
cool exhale of seaweed, tide pools, rock
jagged edges along rugged shores, surge
breaks, listen to pocketknife whistles of
gulls at low tide
imagine this scientist looking
leaning, observing with sandpaper palms
as the sea hums secrets
as songbirds warble
witchery, witchery

she wrote *there may be consequences*
when we interfere with nature

toxic masculine atom split
nuclear fallout of chemical industry cries:
what unmarried childless female cares about the
future (she raised three children, ~~does it matter~~)
too emotional too hysterical
to notice fog trucks and dust squads
spraying insecticide confetti with singsong cheer
in parks, on beaches, schools, and streets
"*Good for meeeeeeee*" but not for the
songbirds or salmon

maybe not for you or me either
she wrote *because we just do not know*

what affect they may have
Ms. Carson suggested,
years from now in mothers' milk
in babies' teeth
the world could not ignore the
open wounds left by low tides
infants born with hands on top of their
shoulders, trunks sprouted with little
feet, how much longer can we conceal
what we do to the air, water, and trees

we do to us, how much longer of
profits over people
how long does it take to break down
Ms. Carson persisted
for this
pitch forks raised to
break her
like the eagles' thin
chemical-cracked eggshells

if she could take a big yellow taxi
here, she could see
not much has changed
not much has changed
still foolish manufactured boundaries
politics, poison sprays

what can we do we would ask her other
than help our children wonder show them
how
to pay attention
to leaves who curl up
their edges
like teacups before it rains

would she say, *yes, this exactly*
show them why it is *the most*
important thing
when the hummingbird, oriole, bobwhite
sing *witchery, witchery* each
symphonic spring

[SEO] Survival News Blog:
How to Start a Fire Without a Lighter.
10 Steps (Avg. Monthly Searches, 1,600K)

Zorina Exie Frey

1.   Tread across the water.
   Find a place of peace
   where people aren't minding your business.

Where you're mining for business.

  & trees whisper water &
water drinks trees.

2.   Separate the two,
   the water from the wood.

Separate me from my roots.

3.   Uproot them.
   Pull & tug them from the earth.
   Cut what they hold fast to: roots so deep,
   the dirt swallows them as an earthy secret. Then
   strip their bark until you see white.

Strip my Black until I adopt white.

4.   Set them out to weather.
   Watch its fruit & branches whither.

Watch me zombie.

5.   Break.

Enjoy . . .

6.   Separate them from live wood.
     Sell them in bundles.

Sell my people in bundles.

     Use them
     to build, to cook food,
     as cleaning tools, to thaw icy Settler's hearts.

Use us to build, to cook food, as "The Help."

7.   Watch them go back to ashes,
     back to dust, to earth,
     back to their roots.

This is how death saps untethered.

8.   Rub them together for friction until they heat.
     They steam. They're agitated. You're frustrated.
     They're warm. We're hot.
     We huff. You puff at our resilience
     until we smolder
     red-eyed embers of resentment.

9.   Feed our parish with crack
     until we fight a war on drugs,   *and birth Hip-Hop culture.*
     a combustible explosive
     synergy you covet to control
     but get burned. Ego will hurt.

10. Steep.

     Now, look at what you've done.
                    Look how fierce I've become.

Pride
Tess Kay

of course I can feel their eyes
every time I step outside
they stare
then cross their heart
and rush away shouting why
what should I say when I do not know
what should I do
cover myself head to toe
hide in a hole that they so thoughtfully dug out for me
or climb the highest mountain
and, trembling, try to catch the wind
that escapes through the holes in my palms
yes, time is running out
but we are standing tall
waiting for the storm
because
there is no rainbow without rain

Boxing Day
Emily Decker

After leftovers, we broke down the cardboard casings
of Christmas morning and carted them outside,
piling them next to the fire pit.
The ashes from the last bonfire
had mixed with the Georgia clay
and frozen into a reddish marbled slab.

An army-green dog toy had wedged against
the cindered block, gnawed side up. A bad toss
after too much of everything, probably.
Left alone with the matches, I started with the smaller boxes—
the ones with bits of glittered tags, ribbon spirals, and reindeer
wrapping, scotch-taped and still clinging to the seams.

I hoped they would burn differently, maybe with a pop
and sparkle, before the edges blackened and curled
into themselves. But the wind picked up
and carried them, smoldering, over the fence,
and they settled like gray lace shrouds
on the neighbor's holly bush.

Nothing went up in flames,
but I bundled the rest of the boxes
into the recycling bin anyway and lugged it
to the curb. Mugs of spiked cider appeared.
We circled around the growing warmth
and shifted from foot to foot

until we decided it was time for more—
more leftovers, more naps,
more wondering where to put it all.
I picked up my niece, bundled in fleece, chattering,
smelling of baby powder and smoke,
and I thought about the boxes,

what they had held—
        slippers and bourbon and books
        and dinosaurs and pearls and pink tractors
        and cards with gift cards and all that was asked for—
and what they could have held or never needed to hold.
Burning them suddenly seemed like a better end than reuse.

The ashes would richen the soil and from it,
what better abundance than
        spring's green onions and irises,
        or summer's okra and cherry tomatoes,
        or fall's acorns and squashes
        or next winter's holly branches?

But as we shuffled inside, toddler's mittens
scratched my cheeks as she pulled my face to hers—
sticky and sweet with a secret to tell me—and I knew
every box I ever give her must hold everything
        and more
        and more.

History Cultivates Itself
Ellen Zhang

There is no time to be insecure. *What does*
that say about sacrifice—the only word
you know viscerally. Clogging in capillaries.
Waterfalls grow water. Light cuts light.

Never the same twice. *Isn't that how you justify*
leaving—for something more just. Apples to
oranges from trees to bins from labor to labor.
All this coordination. Despite this, there is slumber.

Significant next to absolutely nothing.
Meshes in fishing nets. Swallow ocean water. Part
regret and disappointment. Only some things
worth keeping. Not bicycles, not winter coats.

So much left behind when there is migration.
Think monarch butterflies taking in milkweed
to survive. *Is this not the same but inherent—*
melanin oxidizing through skin. Act of letting go.

Close your eyes. See diffusion of pollen. Air
hangs heavy with intentionality, remnants
in dreams, from sin to fire. Chemicals
cling onto jeans, fingernails, pores.

Nobody is asking, figuring it out. That is
the beginning of every tragedy. The same way
everyone is involved. *Give me something more*
than this—demands snag on branches.

Migrants leaving and harvesting—Da Capo al Coda.
Melody beckons from betrayal. This is what
the body does best. Every being borne of dirt.
Still this disconnect. *How do you plow forward?*

The Answers Don't Matter
Raychelle Heath

If she never got in the car
If she made the journey with a friend
If she had gone during the day
If she hadn't needed a smoke
If she'd been more polite
would it have mattered

If he had worn a polo instead
and maybe pulled up his pants
If he'd been a bit shorter, a bit lighter
If he'd carried a Bible in his hands
would it have mattered

If he had been visiting a friend
or better, visiting his mom
If he had gone to the neighbor's for sugar
or to the corner store for a Coke
If he had sang for mercy
would it have mattered

If she had decided to have a nightcap before bed
or maybe never to sleep at all

If he had not had the audacity to find
comfort on his own stoop

If she had not still believed that calling
911 for help was an option

If he had just stopped resisting the knee on his neck

would it have mattered

Maybe if the sky hadn't been so blue
or the pavement had not been so very rough and hard
Maybe if the uniform hadn't been so heavy with fear
Maybe then they would've mattered

Safe House
Jude Rittenhouse

A child: eighteen
months but too old
in the eyes. The joy that makes you reach
toward children
has dissolved. This baby's famished smile
creeps beneath my skin
along with the women's bruises,
missing teeth, broken limbs. Fragments I
will carry with my own when I go home
in one hour. Something no other woman here
can do. Those in this shelter's living room,
crowded with cast-off couches and chairs,
have already left what they needed

to leave behind. For a time. For this hour,
I explain how words have power. Black eye
hidden behind loose hair, a woman whispers:
He found my journals,
laughed and said, "Who'd care what you think?"
I ask them to write about who they are
and who they wish to become. The sound
of pens scratching like people buried alive
trapped in shut-tight coffins.

When I offer a chance to share,
two women have called themselves *fat*
though they are not. The child's mother reads:
I am a good mother, but I could not keep
my little angel safe. I want to pass laws
that protect children. When I say
words can call dreams into being, the woman
hidden by her hair thinks she has done it
all wrong. She reads:

I want to be the moon
shining alone, guiding lost souls through night.
She can't yet see
how, already, her light
pierces a deeper darkness.

Primal Scream
Kathryn Wieber

Is it thread that weaved my mouth shut?
I can't remember when my hands learned
such an intricate pattern. Gently now I remove the stitch
careful not to rip my lips so primed
to howl.

A spark is a song, La Loba
sings over my bones.
Although splintered and brittle they are not yet
dead. I am still here standing.

My heart, are you
still human?
Hands, do you still quiver? Or is this the
shaking of fists at the start of the fight.

Lightning pumps the blood
& thunder makes home in my mouth.
It crackles over my tongue and
burns my throat until I am panting from
the sting. My ears are ringing from
the breaking sounds I'm singing.
Ha! – It is freeing to be so loud.

Who knew skin could be a cauldron
capable of such magic.
It brewed this scream, and
alchemized thread into a candle wick.

a train derails in ohio &
they still won't say the name of my country
Mandy Shunnarah

The way the news anchors talk, it could've happened anywhere.
Main Street of Smalltownsville, south of north & east of west—
                              let your imagination do the navigating.

                              The linguistic gymnastics,
the dance of verbiage, the passive voice called objectivity. They say
eastern Ohio, rural Ohio, on the Pennsylvania border, voices
balking at the town's name.

                    Even though it's not east Palestine
as in the West Bank but East Palestine as in a white man in Ohio
who read the newspaper & knew geography from other white men
thought it was a neat name.

                         On derailment day, metal beams and
railroad ties split the town with fire, leaving chemical miasma
in their wake. Broken axle, a penny on the rails, same difference:
bitter particles lodge in throats.

                         Chickens quake & keel during
the controlled burn, but the army says there's nothing toxic
about spilled vinyl chloride & butyl acrylate. It's already flavoring
the water. Already salting the air.

              Just one of many moonlit rides
through East Palestine, but you only hear about destruction when it
becomes disaster. The cameras only turn on when our suffering is
entertaining.

                    Our rescuers tell us nothing's wrong as we watch
our nameless world ablaze. At least one Palestine has deliverers
& redeemers. At least one Palestine hasn't been forsaken.

When one burns, it's not just the will of a cruel god.

Waking Up at the DMV
Kathleen McTigue

That was the week when the final fade
of your mother's mind made you dumb with grief,
dark shades draped between you and your life.
Then, when the car got towed for expired tags,
you were stuck for hours at the DMV, damned
to the slow-shuffle line with all the other sinners.
You started to hate the thick neck of the stranger
ahead of you, tattooed arms, shaved head, sweat-
marked shirt, metal sticking from cheeks and ears. Then
he turned, caught your stare, gave you one hard look.
Like waking in sunlight, his face went soft and vivid.
He said, "Mama, we gonna get through." Touched your cheek
when you started to cry, and you could feel then
again the world, its deep heart still there beating,
with the door held open by his clumsy gentle hands.

A Cringe-Worthy Slice of Wasted Energy, Denying My Queerness
Violeta Garza

Years later as she faced the cancer firing squad,
my mother did not notice me falling for a feminine man.

I loved his playfulness riding a bicycle,
so I pretended I didn't want children.

But stormy skies and blackbirds have a knack for
protecting us from ourselves.

Does my family know I'm queer?
My bike-enthusiast-ex-husband does.

From her realm, my mother knows, too.
She releases me from blame, and places acceptance on a platter.

OFF-GRID
Helen Chen

I am thinking about 188 possibilities. When Baba called me
this time last year I told him, *I don't have any pictures of you.* He
smiles into the camera, lips stretched to level like every image is a
curation
for posterity. Last week, he left steamed osmanthus fish on the table
without a word.

Stamping the wall with one person's confession, penciled inside a
shoebox.
Transcribing unfinished cadences. Crackling then crackling.
Rattling light caught
between fisted knuckles, each a shadow of the other.
Baba tries to make conversation with me. Have you grown taller.

If you don't mature now, when will you ever. Every reaction
to love is an open mouth bridging thumb and pinkie. The longest
distance. Pockmarks scar over palm lines, deepening into the skin.
It circulated around the coastal provinces. Where sea meets foreign
land,

a place called Beautiful Country. Lush foam rushed under the
tarsals. Heaven
swung back-forth. The City of Light
behind you, sun on your shoulder, onto the frame. *Why are you
always trimming
your hair? The icky neck scratch.* Two decades later, remembrance

chews at the vein. Below the bones, breathing
persists. Searching for revelations, what life is supposed to be.
Continuous
motion. Pot bottoms cracking.

37

Under water, a chest is carving out dream
above land. Dependent upon light, I am
suspended between imagination.
How to find guardrails in hushed
darkness. Waiting for spring to last over the honeysuckle's dangling
feet.

A lifetime, he said. Brightness scattered from its source as if
going away, as if there is another
wall to cultivate, where light gathers

Shower Safety
Susan Mack

It's nine p.m. The shower's running. The bathroom lights are off. I know the feet sloshing in the porcelain tub belong to my 16-year-old, who cannot stand to look at their own naked body.

There was a time that I turned the light on when my oldest showered in the dark. That was before the day, three years ago, when they dressed up for Christmas Eve in jeans and a bow tie. I didn't know they'd secretly replaced their sports bras with a chest binder. All I knew was that I wanted them to match my picture of dressed up for Christmas. Frustrated, I asked why they'd chosen those clothes.

Their face crumpled, eyes fell to the floor, cheeks flushed red. "I think I have gender dysphoria," they sobbed before throwing themselves onto their bed, burying their face in the pink-and-yellow quilted pillow shams they'd chosen when they were three.

No. This can't be true, was my first thought as I eyed a closet full of abandoned dresses that were only recently a daily uniform.

But in that moment, standing in front of my oldest, in a bedroom too full of my kid's emotions, there was no space for denial or frustration. I followed them to their bed, ran my hand against their sob-heaving back. I sat and listened as they talked about their dysphoria. I wish I could remember the words spoken. I know they included nonbinary, discomfort, not a girl. I didn't know what to think about it all. I just knew I wanted to quiet my child's screaming needs: for a mom, for affirmation, for acceptance. After half an hour of snuggles, their tears abated enough that we still went to church. We walked in, dressed as we were, holding hands as we sang "Silent Night."

In the following weeks, I helped them clear the dresses from their closet. We went to the salon for a shorter haircut. We bought men's jeans, button downs, and other gender neutral clothes. They started talking about hormone therapy in March, or maybe April.

They talked about taking T and feeling free. I knew, by then, that T stood for testosterone.

It had only been a matter of weeks since their big reveal. I still believed their perceived gender dysphoria might wear off. I'd like to say that my hesitations came entirely from knowing society is kinder to people whose gender matches the one they were assigned at birth. Or maybe they came from a general dislike of pharmaceuticals. But I think I also wasn't ready to give up my ideas about my child's gender. I still hoped they'd find a way for the category of "woman" to include them. But I was also conflicted. I could see how the change in appearance chased away the tears and stress my child had shown around Christmas, when they were at the end of trying to fit into a gender that wasn't theirs.

We went to our family therapist, who had talked to other kids about gender. She helped us sort through steps and options. My kid went to weekly appointments as they transitioned out of the gender identity assigned at birth and into new pronouns, a new name, and a new appearance. With the therapist's support, we set aside questions of hormone therapy until we could get other parts of their life stable as my eldest had just transitioned out of middle school and into an academic magnet high school.

Then the pandemic hit. With it came isolation and a whole new set of emotional adjustment. Just as we hit a place with enough stability that they could possibly move forward with gender-affirming medical treatments, the Texas senate held hearings on a bill that would define letting my child access these treatments as child abuse.

Child abuse? I thought. *Ridiculous*. If my child couldn't live in the world as their preferred gender, I wasn't sure they'd stay alive. Many of the other trans kids I'd met had been hospitalized for depression, panic attacks, and anxiety that dramatically lessened when they got affirming care. How dare the Texas government call us abusers when we're fighting our own internal struggles to figure out how to support our kids?

My anger moved me from reluctant supporter to advocate.

I went to protest the bill. I sat with other parents in the senate gallery listening to one of the bill's sponsors talk about how, when he was a kid, the sensitive boys became the toughest football players and the tomboys turned into the best-looking cheerleaders. As though squeezing into an itty-bitty skirt or skin-tight football pants would cure gender issues for a kid that can't even stand to look at their own body long enough to shower with the lights on.

Every single part of the medical and social work community came out in opposition to that bill. My child and I gave television interviews, live testimony, and spoke at rallies against it. We bonded with the other families, trans people, and allies who were advocating with us.

When the bill failed to pass the legislature in the main session, the first special session, the second special session, and finally the third special session, I breathed more easily. My kid, my friends' kids, the estimated 14,000 trans kids in Texas might just be safe being themselves.

Months passed. Then one week before his primary election, the Texas attorney general issued an opinion that gender-affirming care is child abuse under current state law. Based on that opinion, the governor wrote a letter instructing the Department of Family Protective Services to hunt down parents. He suggested that friends and neighbors should report parents of trans kids.

At first, I confronted the governor's order with the same denial as when my kid said the words gender dysphoria. *No. This can't be real.* But in less than one day, a friend messaged that she couldn't get her son's hormone therapy prescriptions refilled. Another got a visit from Child Protective Services (CPS). This time it was my emotions, not my kid's, that left no space for denial.

I knew CPS was unlikely to open a case on me. Technically, the state's order didn't apply to us. With the political turmoil, my child decided they didn't want to start any gender-affirming medical care before they turn 18. They didn't want to take the risk of being separated from their family in Texas. The medical treatments designed to help trans kids feel safe seemed too dangerous.

But it doesn't mean no one will report me. We've been public with our dissent. People don't know what choices my family has made. They only know that I have a trans kid.

I've programmed numbers into my phone: the ACLU legal team, another legal group that offers pro-bono support for trans families, a friend who works in the district attorney's office. I asked counselors, coaches, friends, and teachers to write letters stating that my husband and I provide a safe environment for our kids.

Some of my support team asked me to write drafts for them because it would be faster than if they wrote them themselves. I searched for the right words to put on the page. Is it okay to call myself a great parent or should I be honest about being as flawed as anyone else? Should I keep talking about the anxiety my kid feels when they go to shower? What words should I write to convince a judge my kids shouldn't be taken away from me, no matter what the governor says?

My husband and I talk continuously about leaving Texas. But we have aging parents who need our care. I can count the months until my kids will finish high school. Leaving would disrupt a lot of lives. Besides, we don't know where else we'd like to go. It would have to be somewhere that my kid, any kid, could still feel welcome to wear what they want, even to Christmas Eve church services.

As I stare at their bathroom door, I don't reach in to turn the light on. I let my kid stay distracted for the moment, so they don't have to look at their body, their state, their government. I'll keep fighting for change until we can both stand to look at them in the light of day.

Tinder
Cori Howard

after Kim Addonizio

if you've ever sat around a table full of married women
let them convince you to borrow a bikini
pose coyly in the pool
if you've ever let them swipe right
text strangers
set up one-night stands
if you've ever met men who were too young
too ambivalent, too rough
spread your legs anyway
if you've ever been unsure what to wear
how much to wax
how they would hold your heart
if you've ever left your strength at home
begged for scraps
let them carve your flesh
if you've ever let them
think they were in charge
let them think
they could
and if you
let yourself believe you were getting
too old too fast
you'll know
none of it's true
listen
we are all alone in search of love
don't be afraid
your time is coming

Kindling
Nancy Huggett

I storm out of the house. This mothering life
a little stick cage—one bundle of needs after another
basketed into my arms, until, flinging them open,
I drop the lot on the welcome mat that needs
vacuuming. Glare at the maple daring to turn red, quicken
my stride to drive the *fuck-off* out of my system. Then

       the echoing slam of other doors rises
like a flood. We are a river
of mothers, wives, lovers, leaving.
Dropping our implements as we go. Keyboard, towel,
mug, trowel, safety pin, car keys, all the rescue remedies
handed down for generations. A rubble of random clues
on city streets. Enough to call in the clean-up crews.
We wind our way to the water. A rippling of flesh, thrashing
with laughter in the shallows, spilling into each other's arms.

We raise our song, praise our breath, prune
our woes. Gather the sticks we need to build
the nest bigger.   Shaking them all the way home.

Black tee
Thomasin LaMay

for Veenie

Afternoon rain. Mismatched drops
splat against the window, each a different tone.
My hands stitch

discordant rhymes.
The Jones Falls fills out beneath the city bridge,
a river when it rains, otherwise

not much, often murky.
You said there was a spot uphill
where water cleared and there

you did your laundry. But today
I carry what I can to my basement
because you also said, once, maybe twice:

there's a place by the wall
where body workers go to die.
My washer spins done.

I reach for your clothes, feel for
what's left, for bits of bone,
finding only wet breath and silence.

Below the washer's drum, not budging,
a stretched-out strap of black tee.
This side of her bodice

flaunts new-formed tentacles, grabs
socks, leggings, bras, all of it,
her clutch ferocious.

Black tee must have sensed
her kin sunk deep in soapy waters
which no one could overcome.

You also said you loved your body
even when it ripped apart, how your job
felt like a trembling throat, eating

with another's mouth. Yours had lost its taste.
You held all your sisters tight, shared
tips, tenderness, cigarettes.

Tee's other strap wraps
around the spinner. Tied at both ends,
tee is torn

beyond repair.
My hands pry the bundle loose,
lift it up to air and light

when instantly—urgently—
tee lets go,
falls to the floor, extinguished

like a gunshot.
I was told it was to your head
from the back, near the ear

but tee lies unmoving.
A bead of water runs off
her broken shoulder, mirrors

color from the ceiling bulb:
bright red, a bit of yellow. But
soon the droplet fades, floats her sad,

beautiful story to the French drain,
    and she's gone.

Her clothes return to the river,
but black tee stays back, corners blue suits
at Clarence du Burns Council Chamber:

Listen. Her name was Veenie.

Bonfire
Jessica Berry

At university, bonfires became a chaste thing.
Spontaneity ruled. Late of a Thursday,
Flocks of us headed to Whiterocks Beach,
Foam against the gallant sand—porcelain as a bride.

We sat beside orange for sweet, twinkling sing-a-longs.
Some boy I barely knew in jeans too low and a beanie covering his ears
Strummed placid notes to the rhythm of
Waves and clouds latticing each other.

We played in the mountain's shoehorn, an off-the-record space.
Young and cross-legged. Singed tartan blanket around four sets of knees,
Sweat and gravel peppering hands,
Scalded by the bonfire, scolded by the wheezing Irish Sea.

As flirting and chin-wagging went on, I liked to watch
Smoke climb the causeway: contracting like jellyfish tails.
Later, I lapped up the smell from my hair, my clothes,
Reminding me of a rich man's library,

Aftershaves at Jazz Club Étoile,
Wood burning stove for granary,
Dalton Trumbo's writing bathtub,
Places I had yet to find.

This summer, bonfires don't harness the same inexperience.
Humming over scorched fields, screeching towns, our sputtering cities,
Corrupt constables pulling on menthols,
Leaning against your doorframe. Ready to ruin your life.

A grandfather's national flag. A daughter's election campaign poster.
Hanging from the inferno's cheeks.
Blood hot, angry angrier anger smacked back in the teenager's
Blazing throats. All our land is left with is ash.

Sun City: Témoignage
Janna Wagner

Cité Soleil, Haïti
March–April 2022

I lie on the floor next to my bed and cry. I look up at the
ceiling—where the rats tumble and dine and live their rat lives—
and see the boards bowing. Hold fast. Please. The gunshots feel
close. The cement under my palms is cool and rough. *Boom. Boom.
Boom.* Reply in staccato. *Silence.* I pull my pillow down beside me.
It is March of 2022. I'm three weeks into my assignment, and I don't
want to be here.

Thick walls separate me from the street. I think of the silence
hanging in the street. I think about breath living in bodies. I think
of kitchens in the lowlands of Brouklin, a neighborhood in Cité
Soleil with absolutely no advantage of height or tree or thickness of
walls. A place where lying down is still not safe; I am silly to sleep
on the floor, but it is here that I can unravel. At six a.m. I'll splash
water on my face and put away the girl who was on the floor. At
seven, I'll be at the hospital, holding a mug of coffee and talking to
the nurses about the faulty printer and traffic and the market price
of meat. We'll sit in plastic chairs in the middle of the emergency
room, breathing in the space before.

Since receiving 16 gunshot wound patients just during my
second week, I have been unraveling. But not because of the blood.
I am unraveling because the public hospitals are all on strike and
my primary job is to find injured and ill patients a hospital that will
accept them. The moral injury of this responsibility, with limited
resources and a patient population that mostly cannot pay for their
referrals, is cutting my soul from my chest.

✳✳✳✳

Originally, I was excited for this posting—Haiti—a country that
always intrigued me. I am here as a nurse with Doctors Without

Borders or Médecins Sans Frontières (MSF), an emergency organization of French origin working to bring medical care to people who cannot access it. And although I have worked with MSF for many assignments, this is my first time as a project medical referent, leading the medical team. Despite field experience in unstable places, I am naive to a truly active war zone. I am in the bidonville of Cité Soleil. It is a place known to Haitians as the worst place to live in the country, a place described by locals and outsiders alike as a human tragedy, a place where poverty is feral.

Cité Soleil's southern borders are lined by the Gulf of Gonâve which opens into the Caribbean Sea, and its neighborhoods that sprawl inland, blending into the outskirts of Port-au-Prince, Haiti's capital. The fighting in Cité Soleil south is intensifying, neighborhood by neighborhood, street by street. We hear rumors that those in the south are becoming increasingly trapped due to inter-gang conflict and ever shifting front lines. There are people with no food. There are people with no water.

Currently, our medical team only provides stand-alone ER care, and we must refer any case that requires more than basic assessments and triage to a different hospital—meaning almost everyone. *But to where?* Every private hospital we speak with is also overwhelmed, drowning in the onslaught of gang-violence victims and demand for ordinary medical services.

I pace outside the emergency department, up to the admin offices, and back again, trying to capture better phone service or Wi-Fi to refer severe cases. Minutes tick to hours as we make phone call after phone call. The patients who meet the strict criteria to be accepted across town at Tabarre, MSF's in-patient burn and trauma hospital, are lucky. Tabarre is also inundated with patients, but at least they have two operating theaters, 24/7 trauma surgeons, a specialized burn ICU, and physical therapy for the long recovery.

The wounded frequently arrive in groups and immediately, we triage. Green: often minor. Yellow: serious injury but still has time.

Red: critical, color just before black; black: color of the last sand in the hourglass.

I sit on the ambulance loading dock between attempts to find phone service, trying not to feel defeated. *Get up. Try harder.* There is always a solution—find it! Keep calling, send it up the chain, ask the medical coordinator in the capital to make a call: exhaust all connections.

They can go to Tabarre? Thank the heavens, the earth has moved. Now the war against time. Get them in the ambulance. Life equals minutes. *Go!*

Even if we find a place, most of our patients cannot pay for a private bed, surgery, or even an X-ray. Sometimes, even after a verbal "yes, bring the patient" from hospital directors or on-duty doctors, our ambulance is still turned away. We circle the city, returning at times to start over, fighting slipping minutes. For patients with head injuries, often received by bullets, it is especially hard to access treatment. Since there are few hospitals with neurosurgery capability, yet a massive increase in head wounds in the Port-au-Prince area, these hospitals often can only make room for children.

Our medical team is definitely not ready for an influx of wounded patients. The Cité Soleil MSF project consists of a four-bed ER with 24-hour observation capacity. There is no lab, radiology, emergency surgery, or blood bank in operation. Within a 24-hour shift, there is only one doctor, one or two nurses, one nurse aid, two stretcher bearers, two hygienists, and (now) me, the medical manager (an ER, pediatric, and acute care nurse).

The ER is one room in one building of a vast, modern, and now empty hospital, once called Douillard. For 10 years, Douillard was a well-known MSF hospital specializing in burn care. In February 2021, all patients were moved across town to Tabarre after three days of intense gang fighting. The staff talk about how they had to crawl on their bellies between wards as unrelenting bullets crisscrossed around the hospital.

Many of our trauma patients are children, teenagers. It is not uncommon for a well-meaning citizen to bring in a patient found lying in the street. A mother, her pregnant body burned from an explosion, arrived too late. I see her husband's arms wrapped around her in the back of a rusted truck. I hear my frantic calls to the on-duty doctor. I am shaky, fragile, unhinged. I pour more coffee. *Stop crying*, I tell myself. *You may not fall apart. Not here, not now. You have to find a way to remain professional.*

Violence, breakdown of that which is holy, when hunger turns to lead and is forgotten. This is no ordinary war. There aren't two sides: there are 10, 11, 12, rippling every day as alliances are forged and burned, key points are gained and lost, ripping the fabric of the country into pieces. Lines are torn through neighborhoods, markets, houses, schools, coastlines, mountain passes, families.

Balles perdues. Lost bullets. Found in heads and hearts and pelvises and hands and legs and arms. Walking to school. Sitting at dinner. Lying in your bed. In a tap-tap—a cab—going to work. These are all excellent places to find lost bullets. When a gunshot wound comes in, or a major burn, or a complex pediatric case, anything needing referral—which most days feels like everything—I help where I can. Often I jump in as the second nurse. Most of the time, I work with the treating doctor to refer urgent cases.

The compound where we live, beside the hospital, is open and green. Burgundy flowers hang like tear drops among the leaves of the banana trees, waiting to become fruit. I smoke and worship coffee and sleep restlessly at night, hoping the phone will not ring, but I am the medical coordinator day and night. If I'm informed of trauma or a case needing referral while in the compound in the evening or at night, I can walk quickly from the living quarters to the hospital, passing through the leafy banana trees, past red and pink hibiscus petals, and under smooth long-fingered mango leaves and arrive in a different world within two minutes.

No one else living in the compound next to the hospital seems as scared as I am. I imagine that no one else is lying on the floor of *their* room crying. Everyone in our ex-pat coordination team are MSF veterans: professional and calm. A combined 45 years of field experience from around the world sits down to dinner late each night and passes the salt and talks story. I still feel wide-eyed among them, trying to absorb their wisdom.

The national Haitian staff are veterans, too: many have worked at the Cité Soleil project since it was first started as Douillard in 2011 or worked with other branches of MSF in maternity, pediatric, orthopedic, sexual violence, or disaster relief projects. They are veterans of difficult circumstances, of carving vibrant lives from uncertainty. They are accomplished and dedicated people who have a passion to help while trying to keep their lives as normal as possible despite unrest in the country. The Haitian national staff (over 90% of our team) are drivers, electricians, doctors, epidemiologists, mechanics, gardeners, nurses, guardians, stretcher bearers, and public health specialists.

I am told in my initial logistics briefing about the difficulties faced by many Haitian staff on their way to and from work. Because of roadblocks or gang fighting, routes that should take half an hour to an hour can take up to three or four. Certain gangs are becoming bigger players in the kidnapping trade, and locals seen to have money, such as medical professionals, are prime targets. Doctors and nurses all over Haiti travel as inconspicuously as possible, and hospitals and clinics open their doors for staff to stay the night. Our doctors leave their cars at home and take motorcycle taxis to work. The ER staff work the 24-hour shifts to limit movement as much as possible.

Nevertheless, the hospital is perfectly positioned as an access point for the vulnerable residents of Cité Soleil, and everyone perseveres. The ER is still open, not only to do what we can for residents but also to maintain a physical presence in Cité Soleil as we hope to one day expand medical services. The gates are open, the lights are on, the water tap outside the gate is flowing, holding space in an abyss.

I know I can't tell you of the real Haiti. It is not here that you will read of the lights and dance of festivals or where I delight you with cursory observations of the colors and religious paintings on the tap-taps. I can't explain the healing properties of local medicinal herbs or where to buy the best spices. I never saw the green of the mountains or the gentle emerald of Cap-Haïtien. I never sang in church on Sundays with the nurses or cheered with a crowd at a football match. I never ate in a family home or laughed along the beach in Jacmel with a friend.

I never left the MSF bubble other than to get in a moving bubble to enter a supermarket bubble. I didn't learn Creole. I barely learned names. I am unable to thread nuance through my pen. I write to you about violence. Because violence is what I saw and breathed, and I write it because it feels urgent. I write because of the way Samentha's eyes became lakes yet did not break into rivers when she told me that she passes Martissant every day on her way to work at the hospital.[1]

Martissant, the quartier where even ghosts have fled, the place that was a place like any other: family homes and shops and goats picking along the street and vendors with sun umbrellas out and backs to any available stone. Now, the streets are quiet, almost empty. Now, if you try to pass through Martissant, you might be shot.

Samentha and I are talking on the blue bench outside of the ER, and she asks if I know how to say pig in French. Le porc. "There are bodies on the streets on the edge of Martissant," she says quietly. "No one has picked them up. I see pigs and dogs eating the bodies as I go by in the morning."

---

1 All names of people mentioned in "Sun City: Témoignage" have been changed for privacy.

                              ****

In April, our team sits around the table in the open pavilion, cracking open cold Prestige and eating plantain chips after dinner when we hear a sudden swell of shouting from one of the outer hospital gates. We pause. A shot. Two. *Fuck*! I start to shake. We stand in a cluster behind the grandpa mango tree. It feels safer there.

Sadly, this night seems almost like any other night. We had already found a stray bullet in the pharmacy. We had already taken shelter in the security room three times in a month. The nurses would laugh at me because I would sit on the floor to be lower. "We are used to this," they would say. "No one should be used to this," I would say.

We always knew MSF wasn't a target. Neutrality and impartiality are security: we treat gang and community members from all sides. We treat *anyone* who meets our criteria and are often stuck trying desperately to stabilize those who need to be hospitalized but have nowhere else to go. The door is open.

A child falls from a motorcycle and bangs his head. He needs a CT scan, but the family cannot pay for it at another hospital. He needs, at the very least, to stay in observation after being partially stabilized. "We must go back now," says the father. "Why?" "I must go back with the motorcycle driver. He is not known, and if he goes back to our area alone, he will be killed." Oh.

A jumble of broken femurs and traffic accidents and crush injuries and no way to get an X-ray or CT scan on site.

A teenage boy is shot in the head. After a two-and-a-half-hour tour of hospitals that all turn him away, he dies in the ambulance. A line of yeses from heroic hospitals that don't have space but said *we will try anyway*.

Intensifying gunfire in Brouklin and Bélécou.

A church-affiliated ambulance bearing wounded is shot at.

An eight-year-old girl is hit by a balle perdue while playing. Bernard Mevs, one of the two hospitals that can do cranial surgery during the strike, agrees to care for her.

A mother who was shot while cooking in her kitchen arrives with a five-day-old bullet lodged in her pelvis. She can barely walk and brings her X-ray in a manila envelope. The bullet is not in an operable place. We send her home.

✳✳✳✳

Several days after that late-night shooting in front of the gate, Angela, our project coordinator, calls an afternoon meeting. Her face is tense. I slide onto the bench, place my open laptop on the table, light a cigarette, and exhale slowly. "We are going to temporarily suspend medical activities."

We sit there quietly, stunned, each person's mind suddenly roiling with tasks and implications. I think about the patients who will arrive at a gate that won't swing open. I think of who might die if we are closed and of those who might live if they go straight to a facility with a surgeon.

Angela shares that just yesterday, a passerby had been questioned at gun point beside the hospital. I learn that the man killed in front of our gate earlier that week had been going around to local hospitals searching for his pregnant wife. He was not known to have any gang affiliation other than where he was living— the south side of Cité Soleil.

We all know that these events change everything. We cannot guarantee safety for our patients because now someone has been targeted simply because of *where* they are living. We are not neutral if only certain gang or community members can access our hospital, but others run the risk of being killed if they want to be treated. Neutrality and impartiality are sacred and unwavering principles of MSF.

And just like that, my assignment is over.

The local staff will stay on salary from home. No one knows how long the suspension will last. Our expat coordination team is being sent home or to other projects immediately. It feels abrupt, disorienting, like an unspooling lifeline that catches suddenly on a rock.

At the news, I feel a mix of emotions. I feel a profound relief to know that soon I will be farther away from the violence. I feel gratitude that I no longer have to worry if I'm falling apart so much that I can't remain professional. I feel angry, too, and want to stay. I want to fight.

I agonize over the patients. I think about the boy in a red snowball hat, with burned arms. I wonder about the eight-year-old girl who was shot in the head and is still recovering. I think about how I am safe in a quiet place, drinking coffee and writing my last report, but 30 kilometers away gunfire rages. And through this crossfire, families are still doing the best that they can: making breakfast, going to school, catching a tap-tap to work, listening to the radio, going to church, and dreaming dreams.

When I finally fly away, dazed, looking back across the turquoise water, at the faint twist of innocent coastline, I think of the day that the ER will (hopefully) open again. I know that soon, someone else will sleep under my mosquito net and delight in just picked mango and hear rats chat, too, inside the hands of small palm fronds.

And so, since I could not stay, I write to you of violence. Because it is urgent. Because right now, in Cité Soleil, a balle perdue is found by a beautiful person it is not meant for.

Témoignage. To bear witness.

Postscript

In the 10 months it has taken me to write this story, much has changed, and has not changed, for the people of Cité Soleil and for the MSF hospital there. There are new headlines every day and most of the stories continue to cry violence and unrest. The Haitian government has called on the international community for armed assistance. While the public hospital strike that began in March 2022 ended after 154 days, the reprieve was short, as the healthcare system continues to be hit by fuel shortages, targeting of medical professionals, and overwhelming needs.

In May of 2022, MSF France resumed its activities at their Cité Soleil hospital, following another surge of violence. In September 2022, advanced medical posts were set up in Brouklin and Bélécou, two isolated neighborhoods (mentioned above) controlled by opposite gangs, distributing the efforts of MSF outposts equally on both sides of the "conflict line." In March 2023, however, the Cité Soleil hospital found itself on the frontlines of gang warfare and was forced to close once again as it had become too dangerous for both patients and staff to reach the facility.

Even though the context and news in Haiti shifts and changes at a dizzying speed, the violence shown in this story is still present, still relevant, and—in many cases—worse. It is more important than ever for you, the reader, and for the world at large to know the story of what is happening in Haiti. This story represents the viewpoints and experiences of the author as an individual and does not speak for MSF as an organization.

Priestess of Rage
Psyche North Torok

Here's to stepmothers, witches,
unruly women branded wicked or
evil. I'll pay that price, if it's mine.
I can abide being judged.
I can't abide being sweet.
Anger is my guide, my compass,
needle, knife.
Anger summons me to rise up,
not fret so goddamn much
about being liked.
Shunned like a spinster
in the attic, I will spin gold,
a strangling thread, a trip wire,
trapping with web or word.
Listen. I am defeating silence.
	I am breaking down the door.

Prayer to Trans Women
brooklyn baggett

after Rainer Maria Rilke's
"Go to the Limits of Your Longing"

i burn to be in this moment for you,
in this poem for you.
forgive me.   i'm struggling
to move outside the shadow of myself.
the edges are solid
like the concrete it rests upon.
it won't sit still
so i can escape.
Rilke promised god would move inside it,
but i can only feel myself.
maybe my flame is too dim
for both our lives to live.
but know i see you from my flat prison
and ache to make space for you, too—
each day. each hour.
i want our shadows to edify
and move over the hearts of allies—
blanket this metropolis
of apathy and silence.
i am your ally today.
i am your sister.
you are not failing, love!
tell me i am not failing either.
i need the unbearable stories you bare,
your moments of gender silence.
tuck me in and give me blazing dreams
so i may burn to give you mine.

are you the god Rilke spoke of?
are you here with me?
still living? still choosing this land?
step into the light so i can see you
or step into my shadow.

裹上绫罗绸缎 | *Wrapped in Silk*
Chi Li | Yuemin He

第一根白发长出来了　　　　　With the growth of my first white hair
天边因此也生出一缕新月　　　Rose on the horizon a sliver of new moon

是时候该整理一下夜空和情怀　Time to sort out the night sky and my mind
先把月牙移放在柳树梢头再说　Let me first place the tender moon on the
　　　　　　　　　　　　　　willow tip

爱人或许不在身边　　　　　　Love may not be mine
情歌总在　　　　　　　　　　Love song is

婚姻或许不在身边　　　　　　Marriage may not be mine
孩子总在　　　　　　　　　　The child is

战争或许不在身边　　　　　　War may not be mine
危险总在　　　　　　　　　　Danger is

循着江水把心思流得又凉又　　Smooth my brain in the fashion of a river—
　　滑又长　　　　　　　　　　cool, smooth, and serpentine
今宵无别，真的　　　　　　　Tonight, just for this, really

抚摸或许不在身边　　　　　　Caressing may not be mine
丝绸总在　　　　　　　　　　Silk is

抖开樟木箱深藏的绫罗绸缎　　Unfolding the silk from the bottom of a
投入一个完全彻底裸体　　　　　camphorwood chest
　　　　　　　　　　　　　　I let it swaddle a naked me

循着江水把心思流得又凉又　　Smooth my brain in the fashion of a river—
　　滑又长　　　　　　　　　　cool, smooth, and serpentine
今宵无别，真的　　　　　　　Tonight, just for this, really

裹上绫罗绸缎倚窗静立　　　　Wrapped in silk and leaning quietly against
真的望月真的吟诗真的凝固　　　the window
　　　　　　　　　　　　　　I watch the moon, chant this song, feeling
　　　　　　　　　　　　　　　totally rapt

"裹上绫罗绸缎" by poet Chi Li was translated by Yuemin He as
"Wrapped in Silk."

About the poet Chi Li: As the novelist who initiated neorealism
in contemporary Chinese literature, Chi Li has won more than 80
literature awards, including the First Luxun Literary Prize. Her
novels have been translated into eight languages and adapted for
films, TV shows, theater performances, and operas. When her
poetry collection, 池莉诗集. *69 / Chi Li's Poems*, was released in
2016, it surprised many readers. Chi reveals in the epilogue that she
started writing poetry when she was 10. Like air or water, poetry
became something she could not have enough of. Until recently,
her poems were her "personal items," rarely shared.

Contributor's note: I have been translating Chi's poems for an
unusual reason. I am using translation as a pedagogical approach to
teach college composition as it enables slow reading, collaborative
relationships, and intellectual growth. Since Chi used "裹上绫
罗绸缎" to negotiate her own life, and it sounds so daring and
inspirational to me, I was determined to share it with other readers.

Poet's authorization: The poet has granted me written permission
(in Chinese) to translate and publish this poem (and others) along
with my translations.

Passing the Torch of Environmental Stewardship
Michelle Levy

Out my bedroom window, I can see our neighbor's light go on, and I smile at the synchronicity of having looked at the exact moment they kindled their lamp. We share a last name, but we're not related. The two houses to the south are also owned by folks who share our surname—my father's two brothers. Four houses owned by Levys in one suburban block; the fourth was just a coincidence. The common surnames added to the sense that this was a village and the children were being raised in an atmosphere of trust.

Ours was a predominantly Jewish neighborhood. The year was 1984, and the neighborhood was newly established. Between manicured properties, ungroomed buffers became canvases of limitless possibility onto which the neighborhood children could project imagination. We made vacant lots with tall switchgrass and wild clover into our battlegrounds, and stands of deciduous forest into our kingdom's many-spired castles. We roved from house to house in a gaggle, rustling grub to fill our bellies for a whole day of gallivanting, while the adults smoked cigarettes and traded stocks and mowed lawns and played cards in their castles. There was no supervision, for better or worse. I would traverse the fence that protected the school bus lot, where behemoths, painted National School Bus Chrome (a real paint color on file with the National Bureau of Standards), were angle-parked close enough together for me to jump from bus to bus. To this day, whenever I see a lot full of yellow buses, my mind does a quick fox trot for old time's sake.

I was famous for catching the most monarch butterflies. They're sparse now. I netted dozens of grasshoppers. Nature provided a complete curriculum; a stage for my ambitions, a math lesson, a biology lab. My parents still live in the same castle, but the other Levys are gone—my two uncles are deceased and the unrelated Levys moved out. So did the grasshoppers.

The whole subdivision is manicured now. Sidewalks, sod, and standard variety cultivars (maple, locust, and the occasional catalpa) have replaced our wild playgrounds. As kids, we might've appreciated the wide swaths of smooth cement under our roller skates and Big Wheels. Now, there's just dutiful dog walking and evening constitutionals. The noise of boisterous free-range kids in the suburbs has been hushed.

Even though I loved where I grew up, the neon billboards and skyscrapers of Manhattan twinkled hello, and I left our homogenized neighborhood for the bustling, diverse city. I studied at university and made a career there. Instead of trees, I climbed the corporate ladder. Eventually I married, had two children, and paid taxes on my own suburban castle, until I rewound out of the marriage, into a high-rise in the downtown area of the same suburb. My children met friends on the library green, a triangle of grass visible from our apartment. Every week, I'd buy cut flowers to bring a bit of nature indoors. The florist called my building "The Heartbreak Hotel" because so many divorcees resided there while in transition. When the pandemic broke out, I was ready to lock down, but not on the 23rd floor, where the window opened only three inches, for safety. We lucked into an A-frame cabin in a Catskills hamlet surrounded by even more wilderness than I had access to growing up, where my daughters could frolic and catch fireflies. This is where we dwell now, and this is where I want them to grow up and learn in the outdoor classroom as I did.

Here in the Catskills, I let the children play outside and watch them shrink to specks as they wander far into the backwoods. I don't worry too much. They're at ease in the wilderness. We hike and tent camp quite a bit. We sip rainwater from foxgloves, lasso snakes, and let waterfalls pound on our shoulders. We reach elbow deep into moss and build rock cairns and shoot archery on our own property. A well-rounded adult has curiosity, courage, a grasp of taxonomy, and good aim. And my purpose is to raise well-rounded adults

What a gift, rekindling my love of nature, seeing the world through their eyes. On our walks, we wonder aloud whether one day we'll all wear permanent breathing masks, or whether a woman will be POTUS, or whether we'll see a rainbow. Our inquiries range from serious scholarship to wolf howls and hootenanny. I've been given a second chance to till dirt with my fingernails, wade through streams, and roam the meadows . . . if and when I find the time.

Unspoiled environs like the Catskills let me steep in American nostalgia. It's harder and harder to find quiet, dirt roads and waving wildflowers as far as the eye can see. When we're lucky enough to encounter the great wide open, we swoon. By fostering a relationship with nature, and by cultivating a love for all living things, I teach my daughters the Jewish concept of l'vadah ul'shamrah (to till and to tend). The ethic includes not harvesting any species to extinction and showing unerring kindness to animals. To my daughters, I pass the torch.

Touchstone to Remind Me
Katharine Weinmann

a poem found from words within a circle of women talking

Heartening to be here, that's what drew me
to this place, brand new, looking to be inspired,
to hear, to figure out, to carve out
what I need to see, what it looks like
when I need to talk, when we need to talk, to each other.

From deep gladness to deep angst, always seasons.
It's been a little harder now, watching the paradigm
shift what I represent. Trusting in a thread of deepness,
to be strong, to speak truth. It's time to be here
with the wisdom in this circle to breathe
with other women.

I like you just the way you are with your trinkets
of protection for slipping into truth. When guilt
about a burden pulls you by your ankle imploding,
exploding, with no one to lean on out there,
I cry in here. I have a ton to protect this time,

so tell me
it's important: the heart of everything I do
made full circle when millions of heart stones
given when the only stones I have
are rhinestones. I polish and shine them up
to remember my purpose. *A little bit more polish, please.*

Tell me it's OK to say, "fuck you,"
because a well-behaved woman rarely makes
history, and I must lead with my heart.
And even though anything is possible to find
my way into, I'm still seeking something strong
and real to hold onto, where it's easier to see
and be a breath of fresh air.

Ancients, angels, ancestors. Anchors of peace.
Sitting with you there's enough time
for feathers to land, that come to me all my life.
Token. Talisman. Touchstone to remind me
everything and I will be alright.

Root Fracture
Sarah McCartt-Jackson

Sometimes you go into the woods, and you whisper a secret
into your cupped hands. You plant a seed in your palms
and let it grow like raspberry thicket, leaves and stems furred,

furious thorns. You wait for summer, for ripe fruit you know
brings sweetness that you can bite for just a little longer.

When you hear the twig snap of the wild behind you, you stay
on the trail. You move from blaze to blaze like a monk, like a nun
drops each wooden bead between her fingers, each prayer of
    wormwood.

Your eyes sometimes dart like a deer, sometimes stare like a skink
who'd rather bathe on the bright quartz outcrop. Shining.

Look at this tree. Look how hollowed it had been before it fell.
It took one hundred years to fall. One hundred years of rain
from the Gulf of Mexico, windspurs from the Antarctic.

We hold on to the limestone, greenstone, quartzite beneath us
even as our roots split the rock. And we mostly fall to someone

else's chainsaw once we make ourselves a threat. Or a commodity.
Or we are the huntsman who slits our selves from the wolf's belly.
    We take
our trail back however we please. But this isn't that kind of poem.

This is a poem for a woman leaving. I want her to know
that even though a tree gets hollowed out, it makes a new home.

Fill yourself with fur, and if insects eat you, burrow into your bark,
    let them.
Open your branches to a nest and show us all how your body sings.
That creak is the branch of one tree rubbing on another's trunk

when the wind sweeps up out of the valley, plays like a saw fiddle.
Does it ache, open wound? The wind laces through, the grove a
    lung,

undiseased, bristles. You'll find the signs in stacked cairns and deer
    paths,
in a daffodil patch that's all that remains of an old home urging:
    Don't leave. Don't go back.
Look at how a root clutches rock. How stone finds solace in a root
    hollow.

It is better this way: to gather yourself into the river out in the open
rather than under the valley's rocks that threaten to tumble

with any small tremor. First, find a place easy to enter, a sandy bank
with riverstones that lead like cobble into the water. Brace yourself
    for
the snowmelt cold. Emerge your whole body. Open

your eyes. I promise you this: when you stand up dripping back
    into
the sun, you'll be reminded you're with someone you love.

On the Cover:
Doña Sedona (a gradual elevation)
Violeta Garza

wool, acrylic, cotton
27" x 37"

I am frequently guided by my connections to the earth and my Ancestors. It was no different when my tapestry "Doña Sedona (a gradual elevation)" and I got to know each other during the fall of 2022.

I am an intuitive weaver—there is no particular design in mind when I get started. I choose specific yarns that feel attractive or meaningful, somehow, and I let them play together until they tell me what they want. In the case of "Doña Sedona," we stared at each other for quite some time until we were on the same wavelength. The day she and I really gelled was the day we both listened to "The Ballrooms of Mars" by T.Rex, and before we knew it, we were both overlooking electric landscapes.

I used yarn acquired in Portland, Oregon, and San Antonio, Texas, my two hometowns. Of note is the rust-colored churro wool hand-dyed by Zapotec weavers Francisco and Laura Bautista in Sandy, Oregon. I want to thank Casey Galloway and Nancy Heneghan of the University of Texas at San Antonio Southwest Campus—formerly the Southwest School of Art—for their technical support and kindness, and for allowing me to use their Nilus Leclerc floor loom for this project.

I see kindling as the grouping of individual pieces that, with enough chemistry and action, create an explosion. For me, my weaving has been the kindling that has helped me not just fuel my creativity but also cope with multiple brain injuries. There were times that my brain felt like it was literally on fire—it was terribly glamorous. Yet I can call myself a poet and a weaver now precisely because of the introspection that has been necessary to recover. And thanks to "Doña Sedona," I am now a featured artist after she was exhibited at Trinity University here in San Antonio during Contemporary Art Month.

Thank you to the Yellow Arrow editors, particularly Kapua Iao and Matilda Young, for their support of both my poetry and my art.

Contributors

brooklyn baggett (she/her) is a trans poet and artist living in New York City. She holds an MFA from Goddard College and teaches workshops on tactile poetry and rejecting binary, cishet norms in writing. Her work has appeared in *Impossible Archetype*, *The Pitkin Review*, *Big Muddy*, and *River Styx*, among others. brooklyn is dedicated to the radical act of being herself and lifting the voices of trans poets, including her own. Her work often explores liminal spaces of being trans, the complexities of sexualization, and somatic trauma. brooklyn was recently accepted to Sundress Academy for the Arts Summer Residency.

Jessica Berry grew up beside the seaside in Bangor, Northern Ireland. She currently works as an English teacher in Belfast—the best reason for her to get out of bed every morning! Her work has also been included in publications such as *Drawn to the Light*, *A New Ulster*, *Rust & Moth*, *Hyacinth Review*, and *Whale Road Review*. Passionate about spoken poetry, Jessica placed fifth in the 2021 Aspects Literary Festival and won second prize at the 2022 Fingal Poetry Festival. Recently, her poems were selected for the Mono Fiction Poetry Prize long list and Bray Literary Festival short list.

Helen Chen (she/they/她) is a writer based in New York City. She writes essays, poetry, fiction, etc. Their work has been generously featured in *45th Parallel*, *(M)othertongues* at Bennington College, and *Mock Turtle*, among others. She has written for *The Brooklyn Reader* and is the current editor-in-chief of *Writeadelic*, an international literary magazine funded and supported by the International Writing Program at the University of Iowa. She is a current undergraduate at Columbia University in New York City.

Emily Decker, after some time away from writing, is returning to her love of the poetic form. Born in Portsmouth, Virginia, and raised in Ghana and in Atlanta, Georgia, her work often explores the themes of home and where the question of place meets the natural world. She now lives in Baltimore, Maryland, and is working on her first chapbook. She enjoys dabbling in other art forms as well, and you can often find her on a community theater stage, singing with the National Cathedral Choral Society, or sailing around the Baltimore harbor.

Zorina Exie Frey is an essayist, screenwriter, and spoken-word poet working as a publishing content writer and digital designer. Her writings are featured in *Shondaland, Shoutout Miami, Chicken Soup for the Soul: I'm Speaking Now*, and 2022's *The American Journal of Poetry*. Zorina is also a writing instructor for Writing Class Radio.

Violeta Garza (she/they/ella) is a Latinx poet, weaver, and artist from the Historic West Side of San Antonio, Texas. Their poems have appeared in *Acentos Review, Boundless Anthology* 2023, *Voices de la Luna, The Society for the Study of Gloria Anzaldúa*, and elsewhere. She has performed original poems and stories for Texas Public Radio, The Alamo Chapter for Human Rights, and The Curtain Up Cancer Foundation. You can peruse their work at violetagarza.com.

Amanda Hayden (she/her) is Poet Laureate for Sinclair College and a professor (Humanities, Philosophy, and Religions) receiving several pedagogy awards, including the SOCHE Award (2017), Humanities Professor of the Year (2019), and League for Innovation Teaching Excellence Award (2020). Her chapter, "Saunter Like Muir: Experience Projects in Environmental Ethics," was recently published by Routledge (2022) in *Ecopedagogies*, and her poems have been featured in *Green Shoe Sanctuary, Poetry is Life, Stripes Literary Magazine*, and many others. She lives with her family on a small farm with three dogs, two cats, two goats, seven pigs, many chickens, and a duck named Dorothy.

Yuemin He is a writer, translator, and editor. She has written on Asian American literature, Buddhist American literature, East Asian literature and visual art, and composition pedagogy. Her essays have appeared in *The Emergence of Buddhist American Literature, Religion and the Arts, Teaching Asian North American Texts* (MLA 2022), etc. Her poetry translations are anthologized in *Oxford Anthology of Modern and Contemporary American Poetry* (2nd ed.) and published in *Metamorphoses, Ezra, The Cincinnati Review, Copper Nickel*, and many other places. Currently, she is an English professor at Northern Virginia Community College. Yuemin translated several poems, including "裹上绫罗绸缎," by author Chi Li (see p. 68 for more information).

Raychelle Heath is a poet, artist, teacher, yoga and meditation instructor, podcaster, and traveler. She holds a BA in languages and an MFA in poetry. She uses her writing and podcast to tell the multifaceted stories of black women in the world. She also explores her experiences with the culturally rich communities that she has encountered in her travels. She has been published by *Travel Noire, Yellow Arrow Journal, The Brazen Collective*, and *Community Building Art Works*. She is currently curriculum director and sanctuary coach for the Unicorn Authors Club. She also facilitates for The World We Want workshop.

Cori Howard is a writer and poet living on the traditional unceded territory of the Coast Salish peoples. An award-winning journalist of 30 years, her work has appeared in *The New York Times, Washington Post, Real Simple, Conde Nast Traveler*, and *The Independent*, among others. Cori is also the editor of the best-selling anthology *Between Interruptions: Thirty Women Tell the Truth about Motherhood*, and her poetry has been published in *Fieldstone Review, Musing Publications, Cordella Review, Sustenance*, and *The Sound*.

Nancy Huggett is a settler descendant who writes, lives, and caregives on the stolen traditional territory of the Algonquin Anishinaabeg people (Ottawa, Canada). Her work won the 2022 American Literary Review's CNF award, was shortlisted for TNQ's Edna Staebler Personal Essay contest and Cutthroat's Barry Lopez creative nonfiction prize, long listed for the Mslexia Poetry Prize, and has been published in *anti-heroin chic*, *Citron Review*, *Flo.*, *The Forge*, *Intima*, *Literary Mama*, *One Art*, *Prairie Fire*, and *Rust & Moth*.

Tess Kay is a transgender woman writer, poet, and lyricist. She was born and raised in the Czech Republic and later found her home in Minneapolis, Minnesota. Similarly to Minnesota's long cold winters and warm summers, Tess, in her writing, combines themes of loneliness and isolation with moments of hope and faith in fellow human beings.

Al Kelly grew up in Los Angelees with her mama. She lived her life in the sunshine writing poetry, singing, and acting. She has lived in a lot of cool places (Los Angeles, New York, Budapest, Chicago!) and has seen bits and pieces of the world that she thinks are dope. Throughout her life, she has continued to write poetry because it is the most magical way of communicating. She hopes to one day publish a collection of poetry and run away to a country cottage perfectly situated on a Parisian city street where she'll write, laugh, rest, explore, make love, and dance forever.

Thomasin LaMay, writer of many things, has taught music and women/gender studies at Goucher College, Baltimore. She's also a singer and holds a PhD in music history/women's performance practice from the University of Michigan. She currently works with high school kids in southwest Baltimore, where poetry is a perfect venue. She's published in academic journals and a book titled *Musical Voices of Early Modern Women: Many-Headed Melodies*. Her first published poems appeared recently in *Thimble Literary Journal* and *The Ekphrastic Review*. She lives in Baltimore City with about 500 books, 50 plants, a dog, two cats, and fantastic neighbors.

Michelle Levy is a book editor, writing teacher, and nature educator in New York. Her workshops integrate neuroscience, mindfulness, and improvisation. She enjoys archery and skiing, but not at the same time. Her essays have appeared in *Insider*, *Hippocampus*, *Humans and Nature*, *GoNOMAD*, and more. Learn more about her at michellesydneylevy.com.

Susan Mack (she/her) is a longtime Austin, Texas, writer and storyteller who has fairly recently turned from corporate to personal writing. Recently, her work has been published in *Hippocampus*, *The Rubbertop Review*, *CRY magazine*, and *Rio Review*. Her essay "Ostrich Truths" took second place in the Q2 2022 Women on Writing CNF competition. She is currently submitting her full-length memoir, *The 117-day Countdown*, for publication. Susan holds an MFA in creative nonfiction from the Vermont College of Fine Arts.

Annie Marhefka is a writer in Baltimore, Maryland, whose writing has been published by *Lunch Ticket*, *Fatal Flaw Lit*, *Literary Mama*, *Reckon Review*, *Pithead Chapel*, *HAD*, and others, and her work has been nominated for the Pushcart Prize and Best of the Net. She has a degree in creative writing from Washington College and is working on a memoir. Find Annie on Instagram @anniemarhefka, Twitter @charmcityannie, and at anniemarhefka.com.

Sarah McCartt-Jackson, Kentucky poet, educator, and folklorist, has been published by *Indiana Review*, *Journal of American Folklore*, *The Maine Review*, and others. Her poetry books include *Stonelight*, *Calf Canyon*, *Vein of Stone*, and *Children Born on the Wrong Side of the River*. She has served as artist-in-residence for Great Smoky Mountains, Catoctin Mountain, Homestead, and Acadia National Parks. She teaches poetry, environmental education, and elementary school.

Kathleen McTigue was born and raised in Spokane, Washington, and lives in Boston, Massachusetts. She is an ordained Unitarian Universalist minister and worked in parish ministry for 25 years until 2012, when she began directing a new denominational social justice program. Now retired, Kathleen studies and writes poetry, accompanies Spanish-speaking migrants as they seek asylum, and takes long hikes with her energetic dog. She and her husband Nick are the parents of three adult children.

Sarah Piper is a writer, physician, patient, and advocate, a Midwesterner by roots and accent, and a Californian by address and adventurousness. After years of caring for seriously ill patients as a palliative medicine physician, her own illness invited a new course, and words have become a second life. She now writes about relationship, the medicine of tiny truths, the experience of being undone by circumstance, and the myriad ways we can be voicefully, marvelously remade. When not writing, you'll find Sarah celebrating small wins, trying to make noise on a guitar, and dreaming of her next big hike.

Jude Rittenhouse, award-winning poet and short-story and creative nonfiction writer, is also a teacher, speaker, and mental health professional. Her poems, essays, and articles appear in *Nimrod International Journal*, *Tiferet Journal*, *Narrative Northeast*, and *DoveTales*, among others, and she was included in *The Tiferet Talk Interviews* (Tiferet Press 2013). Awards include a writer's grant from the Vermont Studio Center and multiple designations as finalist for Nimrod's Pablo Neruda Prize and the Tiferet Poetry Prize. Founding coeditor for the feminist literary magazine *Moon Journal* (1995–2009, archived at Smith College), Jude has spent decades helping people use their creativity to transform and grow.

Mandy Shunnarah is an Alabama-born, Palestinian-American writer who now calls Columbus, Ohio, home. Mandy's essays, poetry, and short stories have been published in *The New York Times*, *Electric Literature*, *The Rumpus*, *Entropy Magazine*, *The Normal School*, *Heavy Feather Review*, and others. Mandy's first book, *Midwest Shreds: Skaters and Skateparks in Middle America*, is forthcoming from Belt Publishing. Read more at mandyshunnarah.com.

Psyche North Torok, a graduate of Ohio State University, is a lover of words, language, and nature. Her poems have appeared in many journals, including *Common Ground Review*, *Avalon Literary Review*, *Plainsongs*, *Earth's Daughters*, and numerous anthologies, including *Forgotten Women* and *Dead of Winter*. She lives and works in Columbus, Ohio.

Janna Wagner has been a nurse with Doctors Without Borders since 2014. She writes from her cabin at the end of the road in Homer, Alaska. Janna is a first year MFA student at Pacific Lutheran University's Rainier Writing Workshop. She can be reached at janna.e.wagner@gmail.com.

Katharine Weinmann, introspective and contemplative by nature, is a seeker whose reading of mystics, poets, and philosophers shapes the container from which her words emerge. Informed by her clinical training as a psychotherapist, professional practice as a leadership coach and group facilitator, and personal inner work in depth psychology, Katharine writes poetry and creative nonfiction, sharing the beauty in her imperfect, sometimes broken, mostly well-lived, and much loved life in her blog, A Wabi Sabi Life. Published in several global and national online journals and anthologies, she is coeditor of the Canadian online quarterly, *Sage-ing: The Journal of Creative Aging*.

Kathryn Wieber is a writer who is still getting accustomed to owning that title. Her preferred medium is poetry but she has recently found herself experimenting with longer form as well. She lives in Brooklyn, New York, with her boyfriend and dog. When not writing, she can be found outside somewhere or indulging in comfort food.

Matilda Young (she/they) is a poet with an MFA in poetry from the University of Maryland. She has been published in several journals, including *Anatolios Magazine*, *Angel City Review*, and *Entropy Magazine's Blackcackle*. She enjoys Edgar Allan Poe jokes, not being in their apartment, and being obnoxious about the benefits of stovetop popcorn.

Ellen Zhang is a student at Harvard Medical School who has studied under Pulitzer Prize winner Jorie Graham, poet Rosebud Ben-Oni, and poet Josh Bell. She has been recognized by the 2022 DeBakey Poetry Prize, 2022 Dibase Poetry Contest, and as 2019 National Student Poet semifinalist. Her works appear or are forthcoming in *Southward Literary Journal*, *Rappahannock Review*, *COUNTERCLOCK Journal*, and elsewhere.